PRESENTED TO

BY

DATE

Bill & Gloria Gaither Present

A BILLY GRAHAM HOMECOMING
Celebration

Project Editor: Pat Matuszak

Design by Koechel Peterson & Associates, Minneapolis, Minnesota

Homecoming® is a Trademark of Gaither Music Company, Inc.™

Excerpts on pages 5, 9, 19, 20, 36, 45, 68 and 86 taken from *Billy Graham: God's Ambassador*, TIME® LIFE Books, 1999, were used by permission of the Billy Graham Evangelical Association.

Words and Music to *Thank You* by Ray Boltz. Copyright © 1988 Gaither Music Company. All rights controlled by Gaither Copyright Management. Used by permission.

Photos on pages 5, 8, 9, 15, 19–21, 31, 36, 37, 38, 44, 45, 57, 66, 68, 69, 77, 80, 85, 86, 87, 89, 95, 96, presentation page, title page and cover images compliments of the Billy Graham Evangelical Association.

Photos on pages 10, 12–14, 17, 25, 28, 35, 42, 43, 50–56, 58, 60, 62–64, 71–74, 76, 77, 83, 88, 92, 94, endsheets and cover images by Allen Clark @ TIG.

All other photos by Tim Campbell.

ISBN 0-8499-9567-1

Printed and bound in Belgium

Thank You

Thank you for giving to the Lord;

I am a life that was changed.

Thank you for giving to the Lord;

I am so glad you gave.

RAY BOLTZ

My husband had always said that his life was not his own.

His name had been lifted from obscurity by God.

RUTH BELL GRAHAM

The pages of this book are filled with messages from artists whose names you will recognize and whose lives have been impacted by the eternal message and music of the Billy Graham Crusades. The Homecoming friends who contributed to this book came together to record a musical event we held to honor Dr. Billy Graham.

We all agreed that his ministry may be the most profound evangelistic influence the world has ever known. During this inspiring retreat, we gathered together and sang and reminisced about one man who so tirelessly gave his all to delivering the Song of Jesus to the ends of the earth: Dr. Billy Graham.

Music has always been a powerful element of the Billy Graham Crusades. As they traveled around the world, his crusades introduced contemporary worship music and artists to churches of all denominations. Gloria and I felt it was an honor to be among those whose songs were chosen to reinforce their simple, straightforward gospel message.

I'll never forget the first time our song "He Touched Me" was used during a Billy Graham Crusade. We later rejoiced to see "Because He Lives" chosen as one of their theme songs. The message of that song was never more overwhelming to me than when I heard it sung in a language I didn't know from a foreign arena full of brand new believers. It was obvious to me that those people weren't singing our song; they were singing His Song.

Throughout more than five decades of Billy Graham Crusades, the role of music has been directly related to the sensitivity and obedience of Dr. Graham and his inspired team. Over the years I hoped that someday there would be an opportunity to properly thank Dr. Graham and his team for all that they were doing . . . for always listening for His Song. That is why you are holding this book in your hands.

BILL GAITHER

Gratitude

I have had the privilege of preaching the Gospel on every continent in most of the countries of the world. And I have found that when I present the simple message of the Gospel of Jesus Christ, with authority, quoting from the very Word of God—He takes that message and drives it supernaturally into the human heart.

BILLY GRAHAM

The most memorable crusade for me was the first youth night at the Cleveland crusade—to see 10,000 kids walk forward was amazing. His message and the way he communicated to those kids was extraordinary. I just sat and cried. I just prayed, 'Thank you God for allowing me to be a part of this.'

MICHAEL W. SMITH

I think of Billy Graham as God's faithful messenger. It's as though God called him the way a king would call a trusted servant when he wanted to send a message. The king would write out his message, roll it into a scroll, then seal it with wax and stamp his insignia into it with his own ring. The messenger's part was to just deliver that message to someone else. He was supposed to do that with his whole heart, but he knew he had been entrusted with someone else's message. And I think Billy Graham's done that with great authority and great objectivity. He doesn't get all wrapped up in politics and things that are not part of the true message God sent him to deliver. He is an example of how one person who remains committed to Christ, and undaunted in his effort, can change the world.

GUY PENROD

Billy Graham will be described as a man who has never lost his focus. His message was beating this one drum—that God so loved the world that He gave His only son.

GLORIA GAITHER

When I was in high school I heard Billy Graham on TV. I'll never forget how powerfully he preached and how beautifully George Beverly Shea sang "I'd Rather Have Jesus". That was when I really understood God's message to me that Jesus had to be first in my life if anything else was going to happen.

ANN DOWNING

I'm so thankful for Billy Graham's influence in my own family. One night we were all watching one of the crusades together, and when the invitation was given my oldest daughter, Amy, turned to me and said, 'Daddy, would you pray with me?' She had acknowledged before that the Lord had come into her heart, but that night she said, 'I just feel all alone.' After we prayed, she looked up at me and said, 'Daddy, I don't feel alone anymore.'

SQUIRE PARSONS

The first time the Gaither Vocal Band sang for Billy Graham was an unforgettable experience because he's been doing this thing longer than I've been alive. It was kind of like meeting the apostle Paul. He's devoted his life to this calling and done it whole-heartedly.

DAVID PHELPS

Our first Billy Graham Crusade was in Toronto. Our daughter Amy sang "I Am A Promise". My little nephew saw it on TV and heard them say there were sixty thousand people there. He said 'My goodness, Uncle Bill is drawing big crowds, isn't he?' And my sister answered, 'Yes and Billy Graham is drawing some pretty big crowds, too!' My nephew thought those people all came to see me!

BILL GAITHER

When we got together to do this tribute to Billy Graham, I thought it was so appropriate that we sang Ray Boltz' beautiful song, "Thank You". I was sitting one chair over from Cliff Barrows and George Beverly Shea. I looked at them and felt so grateful for their influence over the years. I reached over to them and patted their hands and said thank you. I looked at Gloria and whispered thank you. I felt as if the song's lyrics perfectly expressed my gratitude to all those people who have made an impact in my own personal life and ministry.

GERON DAVIS

When Billy Graham stands up there to speak, it is always the simple message everyone can understand. It is something real. People like to see the survivor type of shows on TV because they want to see reality. People are ready for something real. Well, Billy Graham has always been bringing them that—so real, so simple.

ANTHONY BURGER

The main reason I wanted to participate was because it was a tribute to Billy Graham. It is such an honor to be a part of anything he is doing. A few years ago, my husband asked me if there was something I wanted to do that I've never done, and I said 'You know what, I've never done anything for Billy Graham.' During that same week they called and asked me to be a part of a crusade for the first time. I've done four or five crusades since then. With Billy Graham, it's all about Jesus. He is the most humble person I've ever met.

CeCe Winans

Dear God, I prayed, all unafraid (as we're inclined to do)
　　I do not need a handsome man but let him be like You;
I do not need one big and strong nor yet so very tall,
　　nor need he be some genius or wealthy, Lord, at all;
But let his head be high, dear God, and let his eye be clear,
　　his shoulders straight, whate'er his state,
　　whate'er his earthly sphere;
And let his face have character, a ruggedness of soul,
　　and let his whole life show, dear God, a singleness of goal;
Then when he comes (as he will come) with quiet eyes aglow,
　　I'll understand that he's the man I prayed for long ago.

RUTH BELL GRAHAM

HE'S THE MAN I PRAYED FOR LONG AGO

Old & New Friends

I am calling for a revival that will cause

men and women to return to their offices and shops

to live out the teaching of Christ in their daily relationships.

BILLY GRAHAM

It's been amazing how God has worked in the lives of those who came together for this tribute to Billy Graham. It reminds me of the special people that God brought into my husband's life who helped inspire him to write some of the songs that we have been singing.

Here's the inside story about how my husband, Stuart Hamblen, wrote "It Is No Secret". Back in the 1940s, there was a bunch of fellows visiting at John Wayne's home. During the conversation, some men mentioned about how they had their own private psychiatrists. They were actually bragging about whose doctor was best! Stuart casually remarked, 'Well, it's no secret what God can do in a man's life, you know.' As he was leaving, John Wayne walked him to the door and said, 'Stuart, you made a powerful statement tonight. You ought to write a song about it.' Stuart asked, 'What statement?' John answered, 'You said it is no secret what God can do in a man's life.' So Stuart mulled the idea over as he walked home. When he came into our house, he sat down at the organ just picking out notes with his fingers. Suddenly, the hall clock struck midnight. That was how he got the idea for the first verse, 'The chimes of time ring out the news. Another day is through.' When he was done, he thought, 'I'm gonna take this to the wife and see what she thinks about it.' But he thought I might be in bed by this time, so he looked at the clock and was surprised to see it was just 17 minutes past midnight. He wrote the whole song in 17 minutes! He wrote like that When a song was ready to be born, everything else dropped. It was like a baby coming.

SUZY HAMBLEN

Through the years, untold men and women have come to help my father. They've given their names and they've given their talent to help set the stage for the preaching of the Gospel. And it's been a wonderful, wonderful thing.

The Scripture speaks about there being different gifts from God. If we were all hands, we wouldn't get much done. The same is true if we were all heads, or if all of us were mouths. It takes the hands, it takes the feet, it takes the eyes, it takes the ears—it takes all of us to make a body. And God has used this team in a mighty way.

FRANKLIN GRAHAM

GOD HAS USED THIS TEAM IN A MIGHTY WAY

We often tell our kids, 'We don't sing old songs because they're old, we sing them because they are great and they deserve to live.' Music styles come and go, but the message of the song goes on and on. My vision for the Homecoming videos was just to go with my heart. I felt that there were some older people who were being left out of Christian music. There were some who didn't have a place to have a voice and give a message. It wasn't about fame; it was about honor. I fell in love with that and felt it was a godly thing to give honor to those who went before us. We want to give honor to early gospel songs and their writers.

BILL GAITHER

Ethel Waters sang at many crusades. She was such an important part of the ministry. The first time she came, she just sat in and sang with the other choir members—until someone pointed out who she was!

She was just a beautiful spirit—and she was a cut up too. She had a wonderful sense of humor. The smell of smoke made her sick, so when people behind us smoked, she carried a little aerosol spray and would squirt air freshener between the seats!

RUTH BELL GRAHAM

I worked in New York clerking for an insurance company all during my twenties and took singing lessons at the top of the old Met building. In 1939 I was invited to Chicago to work at the Moody Bible broadcasting station WMBI as an announcer. Until that time, I didn't even know there was such a thing as Christian radio.

That was where I met Billy Graham. He had heard me on one of my programs called 'Hymns from the Chapel'. He made the train ride just to come in to meet me and say thank you. I realized I was meeting a very fine young man. He was 21 and I was 31—and there is still that age difference!

He's a wonderful man who doesn't have a selfish bone in his body. Our first Crusade was in 1947 in Charlotte and I haven't gotten the pink slip yet—though I keep expecting it any day now!

GEORGE BEVERLY SHEA

Bev and I sing two-part harmony to "This Little Light of Mine", and one day Billy got up and said, 'How about letting me sing one part?' Well, we were shocked: 'Are you serious?' He replied, 'Yeah.' So we started singing and we got to the part that asks the question 'Hide it under a bushel?' At that moment, Billy stood up and shouted the song's reply: 'No!' That was all there was to the part he'd wanted to contribute. We did that at the last crusade and the people loved it!

CLIFF BARROWS

The first time I sang at a crusade, I almost got shot! It was because I was so determined to get through the crowd and shake Billy Graham's hand. I thought about how I didn't know if I'd ever do a crusade again, and I wanted to make sure I shook his hand at least one time. They always bring him in right before he speaks and I had it all planned out. Boy, I was determined. I looked at those seven-foot-linebacker, security guard guys and I gritted my teeth and thought, 'I'm going to get by them and shake his hand.' So, I just sprang up with my hand out and landed right in front of him. Everybody ducked because it must have looked like I was coming with a gun, the way I was holding my hand out. But Billy Graham didn't seem nervous about this crazy guy jumping out of the crowd. He just smiled and shook my hand!

MARK LOWRY

Truly great men like Billy Graham and Bill Gaither aren't afraid to admit they are human. Bill Gaither's brain is like a 24-track recorder—but even he can only play one track at a time. Sometimes he will mentally switch tracks in the middle of a song or a conversation. He will just go to something else or someone else. Once he was talking to a visitor and when he switched tracks like that, the man was offended. He wrote and said something like, 'I know you are busy man, but I was in the middle of telling you something that was very important to me, and you just walked off.' Well Bill felt terrible about it and really couldn't remember doing it. So he was trying to think of how to apologize when Gloria heard about it. She said, 'Let me answer that letter.' So she wrote back: 'I know just how you feel and I've put up with that for thirty years. If you think of a solution, please let me know. Your understanding friend, Gloria.'

GERON DAVIS

Looking back, I think of Cliff and Bev Shea and the various people who have worked with my father—how they have prayed for Daddy and have backed him. There were times that he was discouraged like anyone else might be, but their faithful friendship was always such an encouragement.

FRANKLIN GRAHAM

A Homecoming gathering would be the place to be just before the Lord comes back! It's just a little step closer to heaven. I was blessed by every song—it was like the words were new to me! I kept thinking of that passage in Scripture about coming to the wedding feast. I could see that pure joy on everyone's face and felt that sense of communion. It seemed like the Lord was lifting up the curtain and giving us a glimpse of heaven.

EVIE KARLSSON

The Graham and Gaither ministries are made up of a nucleus of people who love God. They aren't potted plants. They have roots that reach deep into the soil. And those roots have embraced substance— they are wrapped around rocks of faith that cannot be shaken. Even though there might be a twenty or thirty-year age span among us, we all grow from the same roots. I think it was such a blessing to be with people who have substance, reach, and depth.

ANDRAÉ CROUCH

There are some things that just can't be tied down by this earth. Though the death of a loved one is an emotional time, there needs to be a healthy theology of dying when a saint goes home. Saints should go out with a celebration party. When our theology about dying is healthy, our theology about living will be fantastic.

BILL GAITHER

> *So many people we've bonded with have gone home to be with Jesus.* It's made us realize that the veil between this world and the next is very sheer! The veil is Christ Himself.
>
> GLORIA GAITHER

Unity

If we are going to touch the people of our communities,

we too must know their sorrows, feel for them

in their temptations, stand with them in their heartbreaks.

BILLY GRAHAM

Music can be uniting and music can be divisive because we all have our style preference. People say: 'This kind of music speaks to me and this other kind of music doesn't.' One of the things we have tried to do in the videos is to bring both young and old folks together and say; 'It's not the music; it's the Spirit of the Lord that draws us together.' We say we have a lot more that unites us than divides us. Even language barriers are broken down by music. I remember seeing one Billy Graham crusade broadcast in China where they were singing a song Gloria and I wrote titled "Because He Lives" translated into Chinese. I was so excited that I called Gloria and said, 'Honey, they are singing our song!'

BILL GAITHER

BARRIERS ARE BROKEN DOWN

The Graham and Gaither ministries continue to blaze a trail outside of the traditional comfort zone. Even early on, they went out of their way to do special things for the youth. Music is always going to change. There isn't any style that God can't use. More than anything, it's the motive of the person who is being used to make that music.

EVIE KARLSSON

In the end, I hope they'll be able to write on our tombstone: 'They gave themselves away for things that mattered.' I'm 55, so I'm half worn out—I wonder what I would be saving myself for anyway? We just hope to have left some tools here that will help people focus on Christ.

GLORIA GAITHER

It's such a blessing when it's some of us lesser lights that God decides to use instead of the bigger stars, so to speak. It's amazing how none of this is rehearsed. It just happens. God decides to use someone and Bill is there to allow it to happen. I don't think that Bill Gaither really knows what's going to happen when we start one of these things.

JAKE HESS

IT'S SUCH A BLESSING

There's such a need for community. Just to get together and fellowship. Once we went for pizza with my kids and my parents—we had fun and made a mess at the tables. When we got back to the car, Dad said, 'It doesn't really take that much to have a good time, does it?' Homecomings are like that day. There are so many divisive things in life, but there is nothing divisive about getting around the piano and singing. Genuine hope, not hype. Some songs put things in perspective. They say that life is not nearly as bad as we think or as good as we think. The secret is to find balance. There is an honest, realistic hope here.

BILL GAITHER

My father wants to be able to bring evangelists here from other parts of the world and be able to just sit down with them and say, 'Here is what God has done through my ministry. Here's what I have learned, and I want to share it with you, so that God will use this to strengthen your ministries and help you in your preaching.'

FRANKLIN GRAHAM

The
Ministry of Song

God has not promised to bless my thoughts,

but He has promised to bless His Word.

BILLY GRAHAM

Gloria and I were married in 1963 and started writing together—I wrote some songs before we met, but I wrote my better songs after she and I got together! One of our goals was to hear one of our songs sung on a Billy Graham crusade telecast. Three years later, we were participating in our first Billy Graham crusade in Toronto. When Cliff Barrows was introducing us, he told the audience: ' "Because He Lives" is Dr. Graham's favorite song.' Then Billy Graham got up from his seat and came over to where I was sitting and said, 'He's not kidding—that's my favorite song!' That was a great moment.

BILL GAITHER

I love great lyrics and great poetry. "The King Is Coming" is one of my favorite songs. When my mother was dying that's the only hymn she requested when we asked her what songs we could put on tape for her to listen to.

RUTH BELL GRAHAM

I LOVE GREAT LYRICS

POETRY

BECAUSE HE LIVES

Music is a way to soften the heart so the word can reach into someone's soul. It's a doorway to the soul. It's a vehicle for the message of the lyric. "Because He Lives" is a favorite of mine. There's not another song that comes close to it. And it's Dr. Graham's favorite, too.

EVIE KARLSSON

Dr. Graham always said how much he appreciates the ministry of music. He says he feels like preaching when Bev gets through singing. He's always mentioned how it prepares his heart like nothing else.

CLIFF BARROWS

When words are set to music, they are the most powerful tools we have. I remember being eight years old and sitting in church the first time I heard a song that resonated so deeply in me— it was like God had created an anchor in my life. Through the rest of my life when I'd hear that song, I could sense that anchor holding deep in my heart—no matter how far I'd drifted from God's way. It was like when I was dating Tori and we had a song that was 'our song'. It's the same way with these gospel songs. They are like God's love song to us. When sermons and friends can't reach us, a song can.

RUSS TAFF

We *have two sets of ears: our physical ears and our spiritual ears.* Music is not only heard by our physical ears, but it is heard by the soul inside of us—by that second set of ears that grasps the spiritual.

JUDY NELON

Music is a very special thing. When you combine
it with the Word of God, the music goes past the
ears and into the heart. Worship music takes you
into His presence. My aim as a gospel singer is to
usher people into the presence of the Lord. I hope
to make people aware of God who have never felt
His love before.

CeCe Winans

There are people who will listen to a gospel song even when they will not listen to a spoken message about the Gospel. If the song they hear is rooted in the Word of God, the hard ground in their heart may be softened to the point that they will be willing to hear a spoken message. Then the music has done the first work in bringing a soul to Jesus.

LILLIE KNAULS

Is the music the point? No. Are expert musicians the point? No. Are great lyrics the point? No. Even the Bible itself as a printed page is not the point. Jesus, the Living Word, is the point.

GLORIA GAITHER

I really love it when Bev Shea sings, "How Great Thou Art". I have an 84-year-old father who loves that song. It's his favorite song in the world. But he doesn't ever get the title right! He always says, 'I love that song, "How Great They Are".' It's one of those endearing things about my father that makes me smile. But I must tell you that even though my father calls the song by the wrong name, he always lives his life to reflect the song's theme that we serve a great big God.

Sue Dodge

It's great talking about these old songs. I never planned this life. I never thought I'd receive a letter from Billy Graham saying 'Come and join us and be our soloist.' The first song I performed was "I Will Sing the Wondrous Story". Billy's mother phoned me the next day and thanked me. And all during her life she'd remember that song and want me to sing it.

GEORGE BEVERLY SHEA

I think it's a toss up whether music makes history or history makes music.

SUZY HAMBLEN

A song has a way of expressing where a person is in his life. It can be about the wishes and the wants of a person, or their victories and defeats. A song tells where we have come from and where we are going, and what we hope to do. How the flame got kindled in our hearts and how it continues to stay burning. In my church we go back and play some of the old songs so the kids know where we have come from. We want to always remember those songs and songwriters God has used. We give honor to the people who have gone before us and shared their wisdom. We never, ever forget them.

ANDRAÉ CROUCH

The wedding of lyrics and melody, especially one that contains the truth of the Gospel, is one of the greatest gifts we'll ever have. The combination of music and poetry can forever transform the listener.

BUDDY GREENE

I remember years back when Cliff Barrows called and asked if the Cathedral Quartet would come and sing in a crusade with him in Cleveland. We were so honored to have the chance to sing with George Beverly Shea and Cliff Barrows. When we got to the stadium, there were 70,000 people in attendance that day. You can't imagine how nervous we were! But Billy came out as I was going up to the platform and we shook hands. Then he leaned in and said, 'Hit me a low note.' And we laughed. Then he went on. I hadn't even been sure that he knew who I was, what I did, or why I was there— but he knew!

GEORGE YOUNCE

Billy Graham is like John the Baptist to me! To be asked to participate in this tribute to him is a great moment of history in my own life. I couldn't ask for anything greater. Where do I go from here? This is the peak!

ANDRAÉ CROUCH

The Word of God is a sword. Music is like the tip of the sword that can pierce the heart. I sometimes wonder why church services try to be overly seeker sensitive because I think there's nothing more powerful than a group of believers just worshiping God. Someone who is not a believer is going to be drawn and attracted by that. They may not understand a true powerful worship experience, but they're going to be attracted to the Spirit of God that is being revealed in the room. To some degree I think the Homecoming music videos do that for a lot of people. The Spirit is captured in some way and moves into people's homes.

STEVE AMERSON

POWERFUL WORSHIP

NO HIGHER HONOR

In the recording studio we were singing "I Will Praise Him" and Bill Gaither said, 'I want you to remember something. There's no higher honor than to know that when you do what you do, somebody is moved by your voice. All this works together and people love to listen to it. It can change their lives.' I thought it was phenomenal that he took the time to remind us of that truth.

ANN DOWNING

Today I had a nostalgic wave come over me for all the times when things were difficult and it was people like the Gaithers, Billy Graham, Cliff Barrows, and Bev Shea who would sing a song or say a word that would encourage me and help me keep going. The unexpected good and bad things that happen are the threads that weave our lives together.

GERON DAVIS

One thing that happened in the studio really affected me. Bill Gaither said, 'You know sometimes statements like "God is in control" just don't mean a lot when you are right in the thick of something. Sometimes all you can say to somebody is "Hold on—joy comes in the morning," like the psalmist said.' It was a simple thought that held a lot of wisdom.

BUDDY MULLINS

"Because He Lives" is my favorite song. All of us go through struggles and feel like we are totally alone. When we can hear songs that proclaim 'I'll never leave you nor forsake you' it gives us the strength to go on. It's a song that's known around the world. It's a rock to the believer.

Roger McDuff

During the Homecoming video, Ricky Skaggs played the song "Somebody's Praying". Everyone in the room began crying. I certainly was. I know the feeling of someone praying for me. When I was a toddler, I fell over in my walker and my hands received third degree burns where they touched the furnace. My hands were so badly injured that the doctors said I might not ever be able to move them again. But God had other plans! When I was only three years old, I came home from church one day and put my tiny fingers up on the keyboard of our old piano and just starting playing it. I've been playing the piano ever since that time.

ANTHONY BURGER

My favorite moment while putting together the Billy Graham Tribute was when Andraé Crouch sat at the piano and sang "Through It All". Everyone in the room began to sing along with him. It was moving not only because of the lyrics that have brought such comfort and assurance to all of us, but also because he had to plow through whatever experiences he had to plow through to pen those lyrics. Regardless of the valley, we have each found God to be true to us through it all.

Janet Paschal

Faithfulness

All that I have been able to do I owe to Jesus Christ.

When you honor me you are really honoring Him.

Any honors I have received I accept

with a sense of inadequacy and humility

and I will reserve the right

to hand all of these someday to Christ,

when I see Him face-to-face.

BILLY GRAHAM

When I first saw the poem, "I'd Rather Have Jesus", I was so moved. My mother found this poem by Rhea Miller, and she put it on the piano in our little parsonage in New Jersey. I looked at her poem's words and I just started creating music for them. After I finished, I felt hands on my shoulder and I turned and there was my mother standing behind me with tears in her eyes. She knew a young man of 23 was still making choices, so she'd wanted me to see those words. God was good to let me put music to that.

GEORGE BEVERLY SHEA

Everything I observed with Billy Graham and his team just blew me away. I will never forget the examples I saw firsthand of integrity, genuine humility, and servanthood. They are so careful to make sure people understand their standards of personal integrity. They leave no room for anything inappropriate.

EVIE KARLSSON

Billy Graham will be thought of as the apostle Paul of modern times. Because of the media tools we have now, he is a thousand times more well known than John Wesley and the other church fathers. Out of a hundred people you would ask to describe Billy Graham, over ninety of them would use the word 'integrity'. That's a rare quality in a world where people in high profile ministries often fall.

GERON DAVIS

I don't know how many times I've heard people express gratitude for the ministry of the Billy Graham organization. It's been such a force for sixty years. Thank God for the integrity of men who've said, 'Let's do it right and honorably.'

BILL GAITHER

Could Billy Graham fail? Yes. He could get off track like any of us. He has said, 'I am the chief of sinners.' When we hear that, we say, 'Oh, yeah, right!' But what we see here is a man who made a lifetime of diffusing heroism. He is not setting himself up to be God to people. He is a servant of Christ.

GLORIA GAITHER

A SERVANT OF CHRIST

Someone told me that when the crusade was over, Billy Graham would just weep and be stunned at how many people had accepted Christ. He would just lie on the floor and weep. He felt unworthy that God would use him to do that.

CYNTHIA CLAWSON

SERVICE

My favorite memories of Billy Graham are the times when we were just sitting in his living room talking. It's just like talking to 'Uncle Billy'—he's genuinely concerned about my life. He will ask how my wife is, and we'll talk about world affairs and what God's doing in different countries. Then as I'm getting ready to leave, I'll say, 'Well, I love you. Thanks for letting me come by.' And it never fails that every time he will stop me and say, 'Well, wait a minute. Let me pray for you.' And, of course, anyone would give his left leg to have Billy Graham pray for them! His prayers are simple, but they are extremely powerful.

MICHAEL W. SMITH

Throughout Billy Graham's ministry, he didn't cave in or bow—right was right; wrong was wrong. He will go down in history as a man who looked the world's leaders right in the eye and told them where the bread was buttered. He's one of few people who can do that without offending anyone. All that man wants to do is serve God.

JIM HAMILL

I had a humbling experience at a Billy Graham crusade. When I started out in Indianapolis, I was a kid with a lot of dreams. I felt I was 'destined for greatness', especially when I was invited to lead one song for the crusade ministers' prayer breakfast. On the way in, I dropped my keys in the mud and cinder parking lot. I was mumbling under my breath, crawling around looking for the keys, digging in the dirt back under my car and trying not to get the knees of my pants muddy. A man came up from behind me and said, 'Here let me get that for you.' He obviously had longer arms, so he reached under and pulled the keys out and gave them to me. I looked up and realized it was Bev Shea. I said 'Bev, you're getting ready to go up on the platform and now you're the one whose knees are all covered with dirt.' And he said, 'That's all right. Just wanted to help a friend.' That was my first experience with George Beverly Shea. He's got a servant's heart, just like the other people in that ministry, including Billy Graham. They'll always be men who want to help a friend they've never met.

Doug Oldham

Both Billy Graham and Bill Gaither have always been true to what they believe God wants from them. They've just told people 'God loves you. God cares.'—which is what we all know and believe. They keep it simple, whether in the music or the message. I was in awe when I heard Billy Graham speak for the first time. It wasn't an emotional ploy, just the simple message of Christ's love. In Gaither songs, the same simple message rings through.

SHERI EASTER

Billy Graham will be looked upon as one of the greatest Christians in history. He's affected more men of power than anyone in history—not just in our country, but around the world.

BUDDY MULLINS

GO IN JESUS' NAME

I've never felt like I've reached anywhere near perfection in my own life. I just live each day and pray as the song says, 'Little is much when God is in it. We labor not for wealth or for fame. There's a crown and you can win it when you go in Jesus' name.'

GEORGE BEVERLY SHEA

FAITH

Thank you, Father, for the joy of being together, for the music of our lives, and for binding us together to Your plan and purpose.

CLIFF BARROWS

To have the Gaithers and the Grahams together is incredibly unique. I would love to hear all the stories that could be told at this gathering. There's a sense of history. To see the human side of Christianity, the struggles with the triumphs, is to see a faith that is real. Some of the songs are as old as trees and some just a few years old. To turn our attention to where all glory and honor belong by singing these songs to God is quite wonderful. There are times in our lives when Jesus must just look down and smile.

       RUSS TAFF

I vividly remember sitting around our little black and white TV and watching the crusade as the people came forward and it was just amazing. Our town would shut down when a Billy Graham Crusade was going on. I like the part in Scripture when the apostle Paul said, 'I didn't come to you with flowery words or tricks up my sleeve, but to bring the Gospel.' And that's exactly what Dr. Graham has done. And I think that was intentional because people will only be able to say, 'Look what God has done.'

JANET PASCHAL

I see Billy Graham as a modern-day anchor of Christianity. He is just one of those evangelists who has never been in question. People all around the world respect him and he transcends every barrier. He's been a gift from God to everyone who has ever heard him or had contact with him.

CHERI PALIOTTA, AVALON

An actor from Hollywood was on safari in Africa riding in a jeep, and they came around a sharp corner and almost hit another jeep that was coming the other way. They had to swerve to get out of the way. The actor was upset and stood up in his vehicle and yelled at the people in the other jeep, 'Where are you going, for Christ's sake?' Suddenly, Billy Graham stood up in the other jeep and called out, 'I go everywhere for Christ's sake.'

GERON DAVIS

Eternal Focus

When my decision for Christ was made I walked slowly

down and knelt in prayer. I opened my heart and knew

for the first time the sweetness and joy of God, of truly being born again.

If some newspaperman had asked me the next day what happened,

I couldn't have told him. I didn't know, but I knew in my heart

that I was somehow different and changed.

That night absolutely changed the direction of my life.

BILLY GRAHAM

It brings tears to my eyes to sit there and watch thousands of people give their life to Jesus because this man has committed his life to that very thing...It is just amazing to me. Billy Graham's message is so simple. He just says, 'You know, this is what you need. And this will make your life better.' When they hear that, they say, 'Okay, if this Jesus is who you're talking about and He's that kind of God, I want Him." And they come...by the thousands.

SUE DODGE

In 1967, some British reporters said they thought it was just the emotion of the song at the end of the crusades that caused people to come forward. So that night at the close of the service, Billy said, 'We aren't going to have any music tonight. But if the Spirit of God is speaking to your heart, just come forward as God calls you.' There was a long dead silence. A few seconds seemed like an eternity. Nobody moved. We all stood there with our eyes closed and our heads bowed in prayer. The choir was ready to begin to sing, in case Dr. Graham changed his mind, when suddenly we heard the sound of a seat being tipped up. Then we heard another. Then we heard them all over. Then came the sound of many footsteps shuffling on the floor as the people came forward. We did it that way for a month! Soon the reporters begged, 'Please play some music—the silence is killing us.'

Cliff Barrows

Hearing Billy Graham preach the Gospel live is something I'll never forget as long as I live. When you hear that huge crowd singing together you realize it's about so much more than who Billy Graham is—and I think he'd be the first person to tell you that.

JOYCE MARTIN MCCOLLOUGH

I wrote a song called "The Altar". It was inspired through Billy Graham's ministry and the song "Just As I Am". I'd seen him on television my whole life and watched him give the invitation saying, 'And now I'm going to ask hundreds of you to come forward to this altar.' When that song began to play, hundreds of people streamed forward. And when I thought about all of the lives, I wished those altars could talk. If they could, they would tell you incredible stories about the lives that have been changed kneeling there. And I like to think about that. Just all the different people, in all different circumstances, seeking forgiveness for sins and struggling, whatever the need is, to come and lay it at the altar.

RAY BOLTZ

I will always cherish what happened in the Buenos Ares crusade. One of the people with us had come to know Christ through watching a crusade on television. It was great to hear Dr. Graham's reaction to his story. He said, 'I never get tired of hearing those testimonies. Praise God for what He did through that sermon.' His genuine humility is what I remember. He is humbled by the fact that God would use him in the way He has around the world. He's a true model of what it means to be an ambassador for Christ.

BUDDY GREENE

One of the most memorable moments I experienced in any crusade happened in 1959. My son, who was eleven years old, walked forward in the rain to make sure he knew the Lord. Another crusade I'll always remember happened at the Cow Palace stadium. My adopted daughter came forward there to accept Jesus as her Savior. I can still see her walking up that sawdust covered aisle in her little rust-colored coat. What precious memories!

GEORGE BEVERLY SHEA

I went to a crusade when I was nine years old. I remember how the rain was pouring down, but nobody moved. Thousands and thousands of umbrellas went up, but no one ran for cover. Everyone stayed there and just hung on every word that Billy Graham said. It was later on that summer that I did make a decision for Christ, and that crusade was a critical point in putting me on the road to making that decision.

MICHAEL PASSONS, AVALON

When my father extends the closing invitation at each crusade, it's not his invitation. It's God's invitation. At that moment when the invitation is given, God starts to touch the hearts of men and women, bringing them to repentance. We just sit back and watch God at work. But everybody is a part of it. In fact, I tell my team, 'Tonight when the invitation is given and when the people come forward, all of us can rejoice, because all of us have had a hand in it.' And that really is true. It's all of us together.

FRANKLIN GRAHAM

Just As I Am

Just as I am, without one plea,

But that Thy blood was shed for me;

And that Thou bidd'st me come to Thee,

O Lamb of God, I come, I come.

CHARLOTTE ELLIOT

His lord said to him, 'Well, done, good and faithful servant...'

Matthew 25:23

The music. The message.

THE SONGS THAT BROUGHT THEM TOGETHER.

The memorable photos in this book represent of the special moments captured during the making of

Bill & Gloria Gaither Present . . . A Billy Graham Music Homecoming.
(2 Ninety-Minute Videos or DVDs)

Experience the full range of emotions in these incredibly powerful shows in both 90-MINUTE HOME VIDEOS and/or DVDs along with the accompanying audio of *A Billy Graham Music Homecoming.* This brand new project features performances by Gospel Music Hall of Fame songwriter/producer Bill Gaither, his lovely wife and partner, Gloria, the Gaither Vocal Band and many of your Homecoming favorites. In addition, you will enjoy intimate interviews with Ruth Graham, Franklin Graham, George Beverly Shea and Cliff Barrows along with authentic footage from the Billy Graham Crusades. This unique collection will become a treasured possession for every lover of inspirational music.

Available wherever music is sold.